Blackout!

Anna Claybourne

Raintree

www.raintreepublishers.co.uk

Visit our website to find out more information about **Raintree** books.

To order:

☎ Phone 44 (0) 1865 888112

▤ Send a fax to 44 (0) 1865 314091

▭ Visit the Raintree bookshop at **www.raintreepublishers.co.uk** to browse our catalogue and order online.

First published in Great Britain by Raintree, Halley Court, Jordan Hill, Oxford OX2 8EJ, part of Pearson Education.
Raintree is a registered trademark of Pearson Education Ltd.

© Pearson Education Ltd 2006
First published in paperback in 2007
The moral right of the proprietor has been asserted.

Editorial: Lucy Thunder and Harriet Milles
Design: Victoria Bevan and Bigtop
Illustrations: Darren Lingard
Picture Research: Melissa Allison and Kay Altwegg
Production: Camilla Crask

Originated by Dot Gradations Ltd
Printed and bound in China by Leo Paper Group

ISBN 978 1 844 43850 1 (hardback)
10 09 08 07 06
10 9 8 7 6 5 4 3 2 1

ISBN 978 1 844 43943 0 (paperback)
10 09 08
10 9 8 7 6 5 4 3 2

British Library Cataloguing in Publication Data
Claybourne, Anna
Blackout!: Electricity and circuits
621. ' 19

A full catalogue record for this book is available from the British Library.

Acknowledgements
The publishers would like to thank the following for permission to reproduce photographs:
Corbis Royalty-free pp. 28 mid, 28 top; Corbis pp. 4-5 (Craig Aurness), 8-9 (Thom Lang); Getty Images pp. 14-15; Getty Images/PhotoDisc pp. 16-17, 28 bottom; Harcourt Education Ltd/Tudor Photography p. 12-13; Photonica p. 26-27 (Michelle Zassenhaus); Rex Features/Sipa Press p. 20-21; Science Photo Library pp. 6 (Oscar Burriel), 18-19 (Simon Lewis), 22-23 (Cordelia Molloy), 24-25 (Larry Mulvehill).

Cover illustration by Darren Lingard.

The publishers would like to thank Nancy Harris and Harold Pratt for their assistance in the preparation of this book.

Every effort has been made to contact copyright holders of any material reproduced in this book. Any omissions will be rectified in subsequent printings if notice is given to the publishers.

Disclaimer
All the Internet addresses (URLs) given in this book were valid at the time of going to press. However, due to the dynamic nature of the Internet, some addresses may have changed, or sites may have changed or ceased to exist since publication. While the author and publishers regret any inconvenience this may cause readers, no responsibility for any such changes can be accepted by either the author or the publishers.

Contents

The lights are out!   4

It's a blackout!   6

The lines are down   14

In the dark   22

Shutdown!   24

Back to normal   26

Electrical inventions timeline   28

Circuit quiz   29

Glossary   30

Want to know more?   31

Index   32

Some words are printed in bold, **like this**. You can find out what they mean on page 30. You can also look in the box at the bottom of the page where they first appear.

The lights are out!

It is the worst storm you have ever seen. Thunder rattles the windows. Lightning streaks across the sky. You can hear creaking and crashing noises in the distance. Then, suddenly, the lights go out. The **electricity** has been cut off!

Have you ever wondered what life would be like without electricity? We use it for so many different things. We would feel lost without it.

Electricity is a type of **energy**. We use it to power things like lights, heaters, TVs, and computers. Some buses and trains work on electricity, too.

Electro Fact!

Energy is the ability to do some kind of work. That could be making things move, heating things up, or making light or sound.

electricity   type of energy
energy   something we use to do work

It's a blackout!

When the **electricity** supply is cut off, it is called a power cut, or a blackout. The light bulbs do not work. The TV screen goes blank. Your computer screen is dark, too. Why has everything stopped working?

▲The lights have gone out and everything is quiet. All you can hear is the storm.

Things like electric lights, TVs, and computers have metal wires inside them. Electricity works by flowing in a **current**, along the wires. The electrical **energy** flowing through things makes them work.

But what happens if the electricity supply is cut off? Then electrical energy cannot flow through the wires. Electrical things, such as lights, do not work.

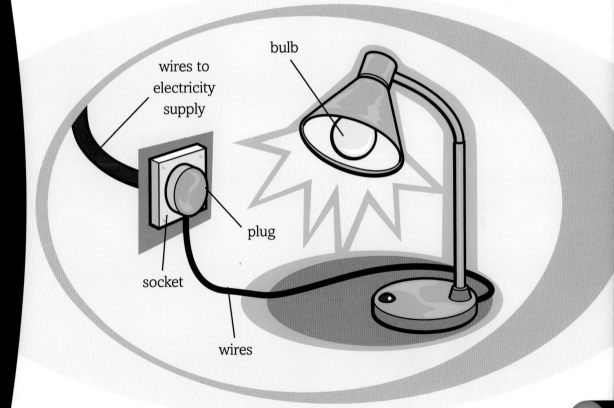

▲ *A lamp works when electricity flows from the socket along the wires and through the bulb.*

What are you going to do?

current flow of electricity

Get a torch!

There are no lights on in your neighbourhood. This means that the **mains electricity** supply has been cut off. But you have an idea! You can use your torch. This is because a torch runs on **electricity** that comes from a **battery**.

Electricity will flow from a battery. But it can only flow if it has somewhere to go – and then come back again! The path for electricity is called a **circuit**. (The diagram on page 9 shows how an electrical circuit works.)

You dig out the torch and press the switch. The bulb flashes on. Now you can see your way around.

battery	small store of electricity
circuit	loop that electricity can flow around
mains electricity	electricity supplied to houses and other buildings

▼*Batteries supply a small amount of electrical **energy**. It is enough to make a torch bulb glow. Electricity flows around the torch in a loop called a circuit.*

1

Electricity flows from the batteries.

2

It flows to the bulb, making it glow.

switch

metal strip

bulb

batteries

4

Then it flows back to the batteries. This completes the circuit.

3

From the bulb, it flows along the metal strip.

Time to find out what is happening ...

Testing, testing

You decide to check that the **electricity** really is off all over your house. You and your older sister run around. You both flick all the light **switches**. You test all the electrical machines. Nothing comes on. You need to find out why …

Switches turn lights, TVs, and other electrical gadgets on and off. When you turn a switch on, it closes up a small gap in the loop of wire called an electrical **circuit.** The electrical **energy** can flow freely around the whole circuit. This makes the gadget work.

When you turn a switch off, the gap opens again. This breaks the circuit. When the circuit is broken, electricity cannot flow. The gadget goes off.

switch something that is used to open or close an electrical circuit

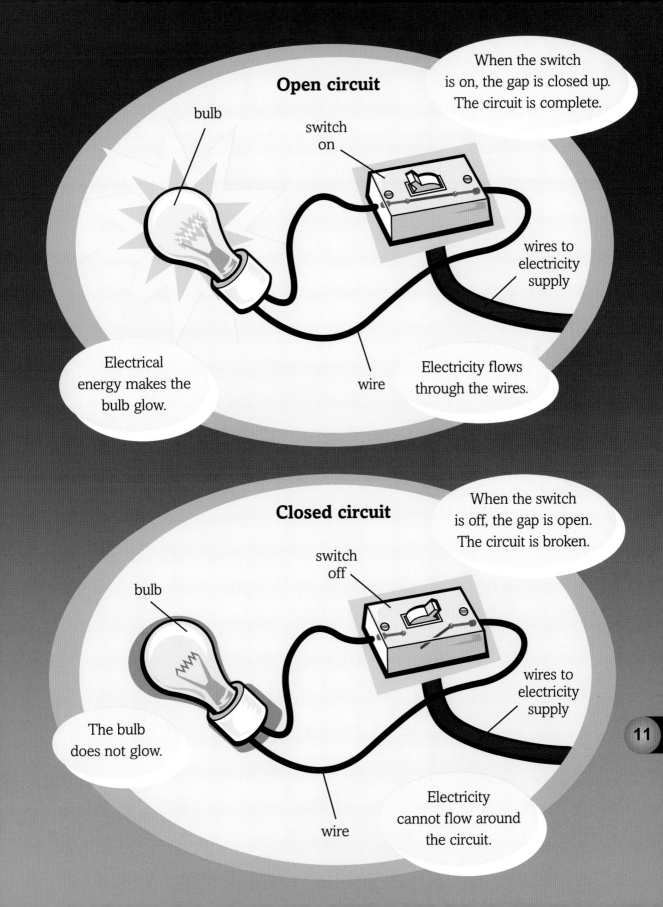

Battery power

Your sister **switches** on the TV to see if the news is on.
Doh! She forgot it would not work. But you have an idea.
You can get the news from your **battery**-operated radio.
You find it and switch it on.

Just as the news begins, the sound starts to get quieter.
Then, the radio goes silent. What is wrong with it?
Oh no! The radio's battery has run out!

"Here is the news ..."

A battery contains a store of chemicals. It turns **energy** from the chemicals into electrical energy. When the **chemical energy** is used up, the battery runs out of electrical energy. It stops working.

Are you ever going to find out why the lights are off?

This is the inside of ▶ a battery. Like the torch, the radio runs on electrical energy supplied by batteries.

chemicals

chemical energy   energy stored in chemicals

The lines are down

You take the **battery** out of the torch and put it into the radio. Now, at last, you can find out what is going on.

The newsreader on the radio says that a storm has torn down some power lines. These power lines carry **electricity** to your neighbourhood. So that is what has happened! The electricity is off all over your town. No one knows when it will come back on.

The electricity supply comes from factories called **power stations**. It flows along a huge **circuit** of thick wires, or cables, to homes, offices, and schools. Just like in a smaller circuit, it has to keep flowing to work. If the circuit is broken, the electricity stops.

When a storm tears down ▶ a power line, it puts a gap in the circuit. No electricity can get through to homes or other buildings.

power station   factory where fuel is turned into electricity

Mum should be home by now.
Where is she?

Stuck in a tunnel

There is a good reason why Mum is not home yet. She is stuck underground in a train tunnel. Hundreds of other passengers are stuck there with her.

The underground train runs on **electricity**. The electrical **energy** flows in a **current** along the metal rails of the train track. It flows to big electric motors under the train. The rails act like the thick cables that carry electricity to your house.

Underground trains ▶ *run on electricity. When the electricity stops, the trains stop too.*

Electro Fact!

The world's first electric underground trains ran in London in the year 1890.

How is everyone going to get out?

Escape!

The passengers are going to have to escape along the tunnel. The driver leads the way with his torch. Everyone walks carefully down the side of the tunnel.

They do not touch the electric rails. If the **electricity** came back on, the rails could be dangerous. Metal wires and rails can **conduct**, or carry, electricity.

The human body can conduct electricity too. You should never touch a wire or rail that has electricity running through it. The electricity can flow through your body. This can give you an electric shock.

In houses, electrical wires are covered with **insulators**. Insulators do not conduct electricity. Rubber and plastic are insulators. They cover electric wires and keep you safe.

conduct   to allow electricity to flow
insulator   something that cannot conduct electricity very well

The passengers can touch these cables, because they are covered in plastic. Electricity cannot flow through the plastic covering.

Electric rails

A long way home

At last, the train passengers find their way to the underground station. They get out on to the street. But Mum still has a long walk home. It is cold, wet, dark, and stormy, and nothing is working!

Shop lights and tills are out of action. Coffee machines in cafes are not working. No one can get a hot drink. The street lights and the traffic lights have all gone out, too. There are traffic jams everywhere.

It is hard for Mum to find her way home. Luckily, she has that key-ring flashlight that you gave her for her birthday. It works with a **battery**. She **switches** the flashlight on. It helps her to find her way.

Electro Fact!

A big blackout hit the north-east of North America in 2003. Thousands of people got stuck far away from their homes.

◀ *Thousands of people will have to find their way home on foot.*

21

What will Mum find when she gets home?

In the dark

Mum finally opens the front door and comes in. She is freezing cold and soaked through. Her torch **battery** is running out.

There is only one thing to do. You all search around for candles. You put the candles in candlesticks and jam jars. This is to make sure that they do not fall over. Then you light the candles with matches.

Thanks to the blackout, ▶ you have gone back in time 200 years. You are using candles as lights.

You eat your dinner by candlelight. It is cold baked beans and untoasted bread. Afterwards you do your homework by candlelight.

It is not easy! You have to sit very near the candles. Even then, it is hard to see. This is what it was like for everyone before **electricity** was invented.

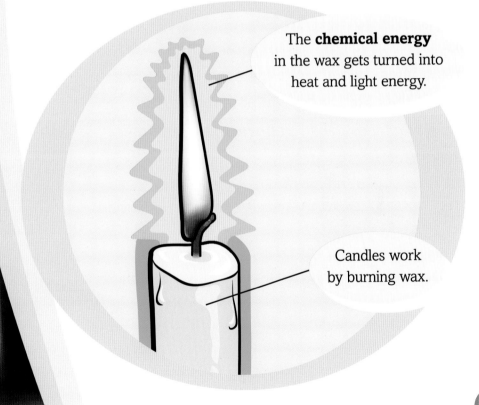

The **chemical energy** in the wax gets turned into heat and light energy.

Candles work by burning wax.

Shutdown!

The blackout goes on all night and into the next day. **Engineers** try to fix the power lines as quickly as possible. It takes a long time.

Meanwhile, you learn to live without lights, the TV, your computer, and all the other electrical gadgets in your house. School is closed. Nothing is working there either. Shops are shut. Traffic lights do not work. Electric trains are not running.

What about hospitals? They need **electricity** to run their life-saving equipment. Luckily, they have machines called **generators**. Generators make electricity.

Electro Fact!

*A generator is a machine that turns **energy** from fuels, such as petrol or diesel, into electricity. Heat from burning the fuel powers the generator and produces electricity.*

engineer   someone who designs or understands machines
generator   machine that turns fuel into electricity

▼The hospital is extra-busy. Lots of people have had accidents in the dark. It is important for hospitals to have a back-up supply of electricity.

Back to normal

It is getting dark again. It is nearly time for another cold dinner by candlelight. Then, suddenly, there is a flicker. You are blinded by bright yellow electric lights!

fossil fuels fuels found in the ground, like coal, oil, and natural gas

◀ *At last, everything is working again! There is so much to do. You can watch TV, surf the Web, or even make some hot, buttered toast!*

You hear your computer starting up in the other room. The fridge starts humming again, and the TV comes on. You change channels to find the news. The blackout is over! The power lines have been mended. **Electricity** is flowing again.

This time you were lucky. The electricity was only off for a day or two. What if it was off for days, or even weeks?

Electro Fact!

*A lot of electricity is made by burning **fossil fuels**. These are fuels such as natural gas, coal, and oil. But the world's fossil fuels are running out. Scientists are working on new ways to make electricity.*

Electrical inventions timeline

Most of the electrical gadgets that we have today were only invented in the last 150 years. This timeline shows some of them.

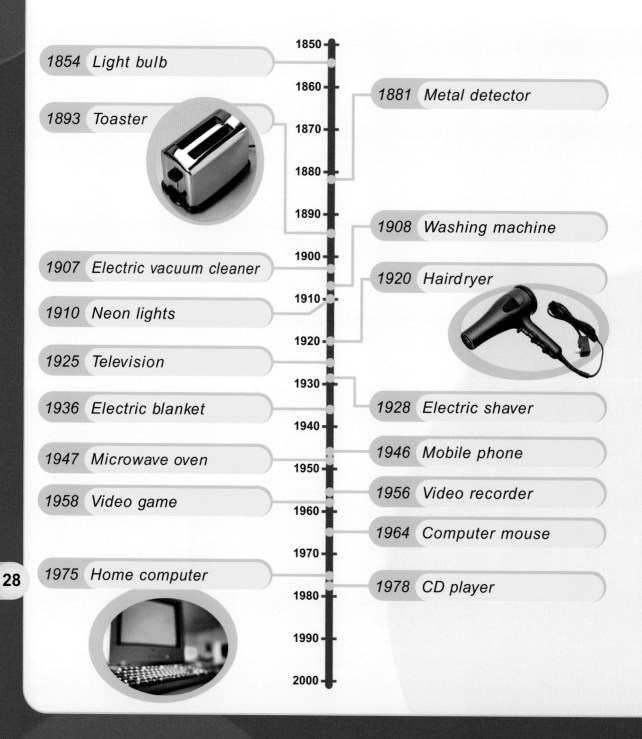

1854   Light bulb

1893   Toaster

1881   Metal detector

1908   Washing machine

1907   Electric vacuum cleaner

1920   Hairdryer

1910   Neon lights

1925   Television

1936   Electric blanket

1928   Electric shaver

1947   Microwave oven

1946   Mobile phone

1958   Video game

1956   Video recorder

1964   Computer mouse

1975   Home computer

1978   CD player

1850
1860
1870
1880
1890
1900
1910
1920
1930
1940
1950
1960
1970
1980
1990
2000

Circuit quiz

Can you name the different parts of this circuit?

Answers

1. Battery 2. Wire 3. Bulb 4. Switch

Glossary

battery small store of electricity. There might be batteries in your alarm clock or TV remote control.

chemical energy energy stored in chemicals. Fuels such as coal, oil, and candle wax contain chemical energy. So do the chemicals in a battery.

circuit loop that electricity can flow around. All electrical items contain wires arranged in a circuit.

conduct to allow electricity to flow. Metal wires can conduct electricity.

current flow of electricity. If an electric current flows through you, you get an electric shock.

electricity type of energy. Energy from electricity powers all kinds of things, from pocket torches to machinery in factories.

energy something we use to do work. Energy comes in many different forms, such as electricity, heat, and light.

engineer someone who designs or understands machines. Engineers use science knowledge to make sure machines work.

fossil fuels fuels found in the ground, like coal, oil, and natural gas. They are slowly running out.

generator machine that turns fuel into electricity. Emergency generators can supply electricity for hospitals in emergencies.

insulator something that cannot conduct electricity very well. We cover electric wires with insulators to make electrical gadgets safer to use.

mains electricity electricity supplied to houses and other buildings. Most modern houses have a mains electricity supply.

power station factory where fuel is turned into electricity. Power stations provide electricity for towns and cities.

switch something that is used to open or close an electrical circuit. When a switch is turned on, the circuit is closed. Electricity can flow.

Want to know more?

Books to read

- *Horrible Science: Shocking Electricity*, by Nick Arnold and Tony De Saulles (Scholastic, 2000)
- *The Power Cut*, by Mick Manning and Brita Granstrom (Franklin Watts, 2002)
- *What Was It Like Before Electricity?*, by Paul Bennett (Raintree, 1995)

Museums to visit

- Science Museum
  Exhibition Road
  London SW7 2DD
  United Kingdom
  www.sciencemuseum.org.uk
- IEEE Virtual Museum of Electricity
  www.ieee-virtual-museum.org

Energy comes in lots of different forms and can be used to do all sorts of things. To see some of them, check out ***Wackiest Machines Ever***.

What will happen in the future if we run out of fuel and cannot make enough electricity? Find out in ***The Future – Bleak or Bright?***

Index

back-up electricity supply 24–25

batteries 8–9, 12–14, 22

blackouts (power cuts) 6–7, 20, 24

bulbs 6–9, 11

cables 14, 16, 19

candles 22–3

chemical energy 13, 23

circuits 8–11, 14, 29

conduction 18

current 7, 16

electric rails 16, 18–19

electric shock 18

electrical inventions 28

electricity 4, 6–11,
  13–14, 16, 18–19, 23–24, 27

energy 4, 7, 9–10, 13, 16, 23–24

engineers 24

flashlights 20

fossil fuels 26–27

gadgets 10, 24, 28

generators 24

hospitals 24–25

insulators 18

lamps 7

lightning 4

mains electricity 8, 24

power lines 14, 24

power stations 14

storms 4, 6, 14

switches 8, 10–11, 13, 20

thunder 4

torches 8–9, 18

underground trains 16–17

wires 7, 10–11, 14, 18